Whose Crazy Idea Was That?

Claire Craig

D0529095

Brainwaves Orange
Whose Crazy Idea Was That?
ISBN 1 86509 485 4

Published by Blake Education Pty Ltd
ABN 074 266 023
Locked Bag 2022
Glebe NSW 2037
Ph: (02) 8585 4085
Fax: (02) 8585 4058
Email: mail@blake.com.au
Website: www.blake.com.au

Series publisher: Sharon Dalgleish
Designer: Cliff Watt
Illustrators: Luke Jurevicius, Matt Lin and Cliff Watt
Photo research: Claire Lovell

Picture credits: pg 7 (bottom) Absolutely Mad Inventions, A.E. Brown and H.A. Jeffcott, Dover Publications; pg 10 and 11 (top left) photolibrary.com; pg 15 Made in Mexico Hula Hoop ® is a designated trademark of ©2002 Wham-O, Inc. All Rights Reserved.; pg 17 (top) Top Hat Entertainment, (bottom) photolibrary.com; pg 19 AAP Image; pg 24 and 25 (left) photolibrary.com; pg 26 photolibrary.com; pg 29 (centre and bottom) photolibrary.com.

Printed in Australia

Contents

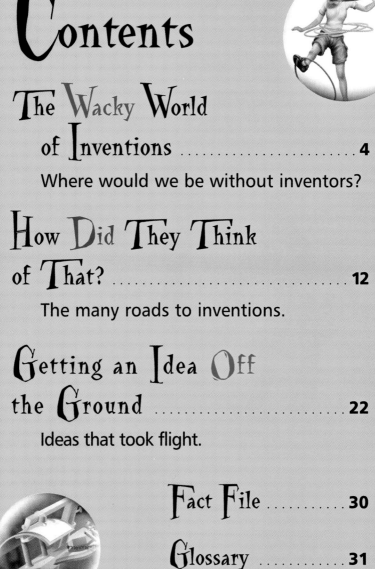

The Wacky World of Inventions

**There's no doubt about it.
Some people have crazy ideas
for inventions.**

Is it your job to clear the table of dirty
dishes after dinner? Then you need a
'dishwashing dinner table'. There's no
need to clear away the mess—just flip the
table over and wash the dishes right there.

Believe it or not, someone really did come
up with this mad invention! And there are
many more ideas just as crazy as this one.

Back to the Drawing Board

Most inventors apply for a **patent** when they think they have a good idea. A patent is a legal document that proves who owns an invention. It stops other people from stealing an idea for twenty years. After that, anyone can use the idea. But the idea is only the beginning. Some ideas look good on paper . . . and that's just where they stay. Would you want to use these three ideas that didn't make it?

Idea 1

Have you lost a lot of food fights lately?
You need a machine to propel food into a crowd.

Idea 2

Wondering what to do with a dead relative?
Put them inside a large glass block. If the block is too big for your room, you can use a smaller glass block for the head.

Idea 3

Do you have problems getting up in the morning? What about:

- a bed that automatically ejects you when the alarm goes off?
- an alarm that pours water on you?
- an alarm clock that hits you?

An Alarm Clock That Strikes . . . You

To apply for a patent, an inventor must draw a diagram and write a description of his or her invention. Not all patents are granted, so the inventor has to give plenty of information to convince the **Patent Office** that the invention is new and useful.

Every patent has a number.

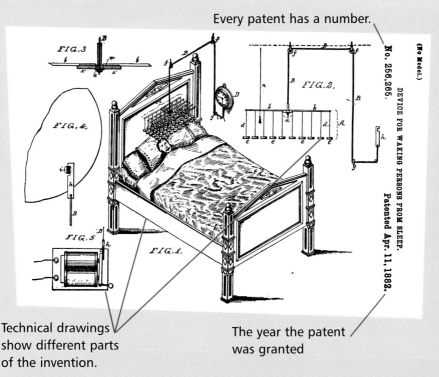

Technical drawings show different parts of the invention.

The year the patent was granted

Ahead of Their Time

Sometimes ideas for inventions sound crazy because they are ahead of their time. One communication idea that people thought was crazy when it first appeared is now used all over the world. The idea was the basis of the first fax machine, and it was invented way back in 1856.

Caselli called his machine a pantelegraph. It was almost 2 m tall.

How Does It Work?

1 A message is written with ink on a metal plate.

2 The plate is placed under a pendulum.

3 The pendulum's metal tip swings over the plate, touching the surface.

4 When the tip touches an uninked section, it causes an **electrical circuit** to be completed.

Giovanni Caselli, an Italian priest, invented a large, heavy machine that could send and receive an actual copy of written notes or pictures. His neighbours called him crazy. Some people thought he was using an evil form of magic. The French government did use the machine for a few years, but then it disappeared. Maybe it cost too much money. Or maybe it was just a good idea ahead of its time.

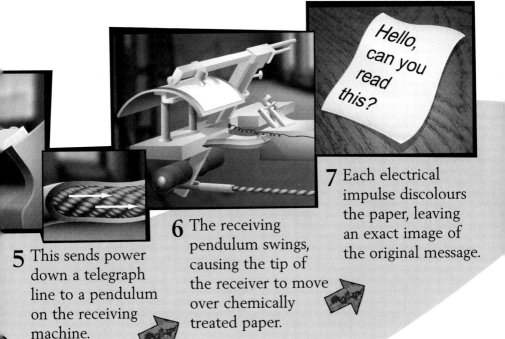

Hello, can you read this?

5 This sends power down a telegraph line to a pendulum on the receiving machine.

6 The receiving pendulum swings, causing the tip of the receiver to move over chemically treated paper.

7 Each electrical impulse discolours the paper, leaving an exact image of the original message.

Bright Lights

I've just invented an inventor!

Patents can be granted on almost anything, from a flower to a rocket. And there's no limit on how many patents one person can hold. One very busy inventor was Thomas Edison. With his team of workers, he invented an electric light bulb, the **phonograph** and movie cameras. In all, he took out 1,093 patents—the world record!

Edison also liked a good joke. He was very famous and everything he did and said was news. He liked to give reporters interesting things to write about. In 1920 he told a reporter that he was working on a machine that could talk to the dead. Newspapers all over the world reported the story. A few years later, Edison admitted he had made it up!

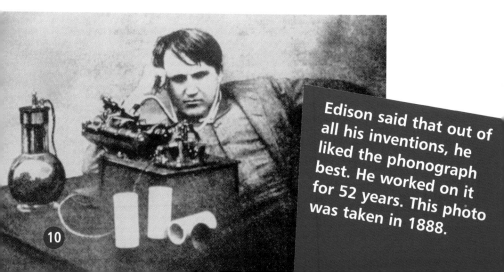

Edison said that out of all his inventions, he liked the phonograph best. He worked on it for 52 years. This photo was taken in 1888.

Edison's motion picture making studio in 1890. The roof could be opened and the whole building rotated to get the best sunlight.

When designing his light bulb, Edison filled 40,000 notebook pages with drawings and notes.

More Everyday Inventions

YEAR	INVENTION	INVENTOR	COUNTRY
3000 BC	marbles	unknown inventor	Egypt
AD 100	comics	unknown inventor	Rome
200	wheelbarrow	Chuko Liang	China
1281	eyeglasses	Silvano Armato	Italy
1642	calculator	Blaise Pascal	France
1759	roller skates	Joseph Merlin	Belgium
1762	sandwich	the Earl of Sandwich	England
1770	toothbrush	William Addis	England
1855	refrigerator	James Harrison	Australia
1901	vacuum cleaner	H. Cecil Booth	England
1902	windscreen wiper	Mary Anderson	United States
1957	correction fluid	Bette Nesmith Graham	United States
1978	bionic ear	Graeme Clark	Australia

How Did They Think of That?

It's gooey like rubber. It bounces and it stretches. Play with it, or use it to take dog hair off the furniture. It's Silly Putty.

The name is a bit of a giveaway because, just as it sounds, Silly Putty wasn't invented on purpose! It was the stuff left over after engineers worked with other materials. No one knew what to do with it, until someone realised you could do a lot with it!

Some inventions are like that. Someone thinks of a new way to use something that has been around for a long time.

Hooping It Up

As long ago as 1,000 BC, children in ancient Greece and Rome played with hoops made from

vines. In colonial days in America, children rolled hoops along the streets, guiding them with sticks. Australian children used bamboo hoops in sports classes at school. But in 1957 the idea was taken one step further. That was the year the Hula Hoop, a hollow plastic hoop, appeared in stores.

This hoopy toy became a huge success. People held contests to see who could twirl the most hoops around their waists, arms, wrists, legs, feet—even around their heads and necks. But the company that made them was not able to get a patent for such an ancient idea. So soon others were making Spin-a-Hoops and Hoop-d-dos. It is estimated that between 60 and 100 million hoops were sold in two years!

UFPT
Unidentified Flying
Pie Tin

Hula Hoops were made in all colours and patterns. At the peak of the craze one company manufactured 20,000 a day.

Invasion of the Frisbees

Around 1957, flying saucers were all the craze. People thought that green aliens would soon invade Earth! Walter Frederick was caught up in the craze. He invented a toy disc that glided through the air and looked like a flying saucer. Then he found out about students at a university called Yale. In the 1870s their favourite piemaker was William Frisbie. They would stuff themselves with his pies and play games throwing the empty pie tins. Nearly eighty years later, Walter had found the name for his toy.

Great Big Copycats?

Some inventions mirror things in the natural world. Nature has given inventors big clues about how to make their inventions work.

Natural Inspiration

Nature	Invention
dandelion seed floating to the ground	parachute
birds and flying fish	aeroplane
wasps building nests from chewed wood	making paper
protective plates of bone on armadillo	armour
rose thorns	barbed wire
camouflage used by animals and insects	camouflage in war
centipedes with jointed sections	trains
beaver	dam building
whale baleen for filtering krill	sieves, fishing nets
rattlesnake's rattle	alarms

When George de Mestral, a Swiss engineer, went for a walk in 1948 he had a close encounter with a burdock plant. After brushing against the plant, he realised that his clothes were covered with spiny **burrs**. As he removed the clinging burrs, he saw that they were covered in hundreds of small hooks. Then he had an idea . . .

Help!

After eight years of experimenting, he finally succeeded in making two nylon strips. One strip had lots of tiny loops and the other had tiny hooks. When the strips were pressed together, they stuck firmly. Today, Velcro has many practical uses—and a few crazy ones like Velcro wall jumping!

Velcro wall jumping

How to Velcro Wall Jump

1 Make sure your suit is made with the opposite side to the Velcro on the wall!

2 Jump off the trampoline and hit the wall so you stick to it.

3 Now try to move about—without falling off.

Hint! For a softer landing when it's time to get unstuck, roll yourself slowly down the wall.

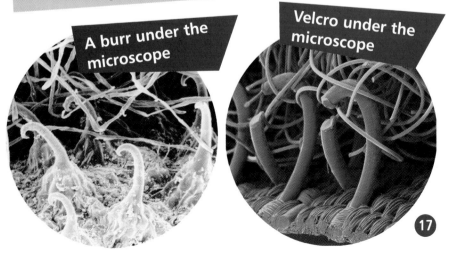

A burr under the microscope

Velcro under the microscope

When One Thing Leads to Another

Sometimes an idea that doesn't work can lead to an idea that does. Levi Strauss didn't set out to become the most famous maker of jeans in history, but that's what happened.

Strauss went to San Francisco in 1853 when the California gold rush was in full swing. He hoped to sell canvas to the **prospectors** so they could use this thick, sturdy material to make tents and wagon covers. But he made a mistake. Nobody wanted to buy his canvas.

What the prospectors really needed was trousers. People worked hard in the goldfields and their trousers wore out quickly. So Levi Strauss made trousers out of the brown canvas he couldn't sell. They quickly sold out. Then Strauss switched to a heavy blue fabric. Today, Levi's blue jeans are worn in every country in the world.

Pants don't wear worth a hoot in the diggings!

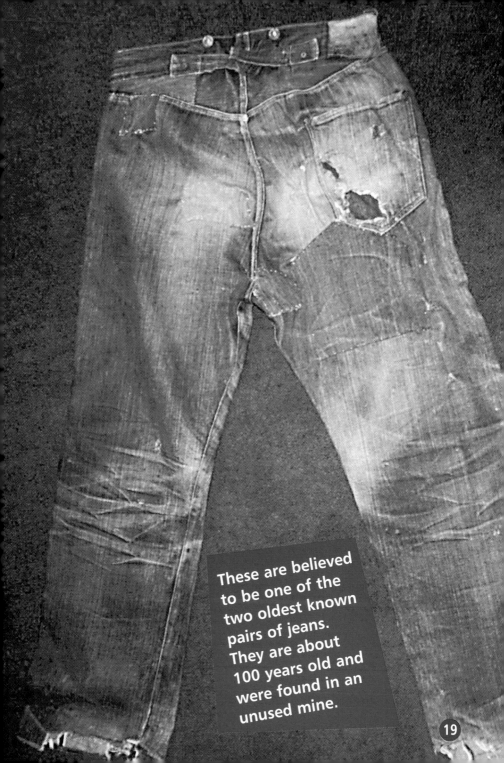

These are believed to be one of the two oldest known pairs of jeans. They are about 100 years old and were found in an unused mine.

Pop! Goes the Invention

Accidents happen . . . and they can lead to great ideas. Sometimes those ideas can stare you in the face—or send a message to your stomach. Other times it can be years before you realise you've invented something pretty good.

I've invented the doughnut!

In 1905, 11-year-old Frank Epperson mixed some flavour with water. By mistake, he left the drink outside all night—with the stirring stick still in it. It was a very cold night. In the morning, Frank saw that the drink had frozen to the stick. It tasted delicious!

Eighteen years later, Frank remembered the frozen sticks. He applied for a patent and began to produce Epsicles. By now he had children of his own and they didn't like the name. They changed it to Popsicles.

Chips to Order!

In 1853, George Crum was working in a restaurant kitchen in Saratoga Springs, US. George was grumpy because he had a difficult customer—a man who kept sending back his fried potatoes saying he wanted them to be thinner and fried longer! So George sliced the potatoes as thin as thin could be. Then he fried them until their sides curled. George thought that would keep the man quiet. But the customer loved them! And so do we.

Getting an Idea off the Ground

The crowd was quiet. The wings felt strong on his back. He ran towards the edge of the cliff. Faster and faster—his arms flapping . . .

Daredevil or crazy? Who were these people trying to fly like birds? It took hundreds of years before people made it into the air.

An Ideas Man

I'll get you one day!

Leonardo da Vinci was a **genius**. He was a painter, a **scholar** and a scientist who lived in the 1400s. But his ideas were far ahead of the times in which he lived. He drew designs for amazing things people thought were impossible: bicycles, parachutes and the craziest of all—flying machines.

Leonardo believed that humans would be able to fly in machines. He studied everything he could about birds. He drew plans for flapping wings attached to a person. He even designed a helicopter.

Leonardo da Vinci was able to imagine what things could exist in the future. Who knows what fantastic ideas he might come up with if he was alive today?

An ageing Leonardo da Vinci (1452–1519) at work.

24

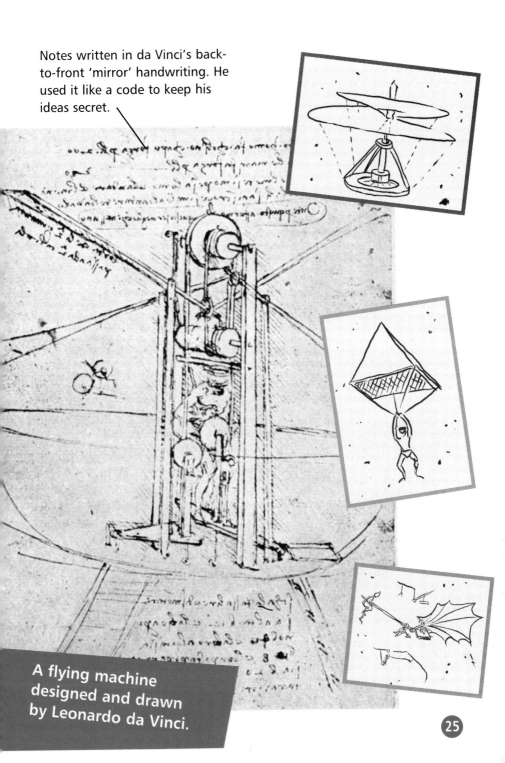

Notes written in da Vinci's back-to-front 'mirror' handwriting. He used it like a code to keep his ideas secret.

A flying machine designed and drawn by Leonardo da Vinci.

Flying High

In 1782 two Frenchmen, Joseph and Etienne Montgolfier, made a balloon out of paper and cloth. Then they lit a fire beneath the balloon. The hot air rising from the fire pushed the balloon up into the sky. The Montgolfier brothers decided that the balloon was now ready for passengers. They must have been short on human **volunteers** because the first passengers were a sheep, a duck and a rooster!

A sheep, a duck and a rooster swing in a cage beneath the balloon. The aim was to see if living creatures could survive such a flight. They did!

In 1783, two other Frenchmen stepped forward and said they would take to the skies in a Montgolfier balloon. They stayed in the air for 25 minutes and travelled more than 8 kilometres. This balloon was the first successful flying craft to carry humans. Anything now seemed possible!

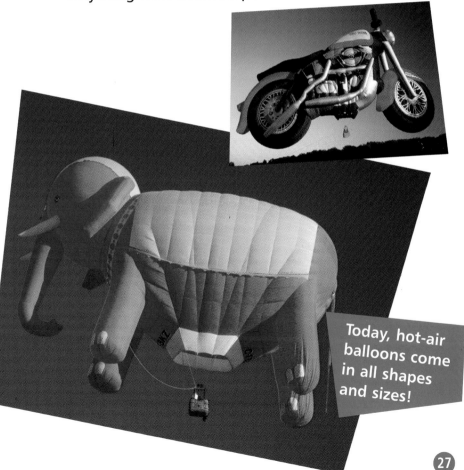

Today, hot-air balloons come in all shapes and sizes!

The Wright Stuff

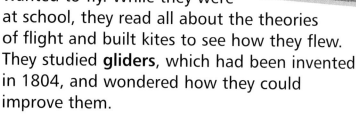

Orville and Wilbur Wright
wanted to fly. While they were
at school, they read all about the theories
of flight and built kites to see how they flew.
They studied **gliders**, which had been invented
in 1804, and wondered how they could
improve them.

They designed their own glider and added a
12-**horsepower** petrol engine to it. They called it
The Flyer. In 1903, they tossed a coin on Kill Devil
Hill in North Carolina to see who would fly the
plane. Orville Wright won the toss and became
the pilot of the first powered flight in history.

Soon aircraft became better and faster, and
aviators flew around the world. Suddenly
the world seemed much smaller. People
wondered where they could fly to next.
Maybe to the moon?

Another crazy idea that came true!

Some of the early attempts to fly

Orville lying on the lower wing.

We have lift off!

Wilbur

The Wright brother's first powered flight in 1903, just as the aircraft left the ground. The flight lasted for about 12 seconds.

Orville

Wilbur

FACT FILE

The first submarine was invented in 1620. It was basically two rowboats with a skin-tight covering. It could stay underwater for three hours.

False teeth were first made out of celluloid, a very early kind of plastic. Unfortunately, hot things, like a cup of tea, made the celluloid melt!

I need another set of arms!

The largest hearing aid ever invented was a throne! People spoke into its hollow arms and the sound travelled into tubes in the ears of King John of Portugal.

The first vacuum cleaner invented was as big as a refrigerator. It took two people to operate. One had to push it while the other pointed the hose.

Arms for eyeglasses were invented 400 years after the glasses themselves. Until then people had to balance their glasses on their nose.

What a mess.

SUPER 02

GLOSSARY

burrs the rough, prickly cases around the seeds of some plants

electrical circuit the path through which electricity flows

genius someone who has very high mental ability, and who has creative, original ideas

gliders motorless aeroplanes that glide from one point to another using gravity or air currents

horsepower a unit of measurement of power

patent a government grant to an inventor, giving him or her the right to be the only one to make, use, and sell an invention for a set period of time

Patent Office the government department that grants patents

phonograph 'talking machine'—the early name for record players, which were in use before CD players

prospectors people who search for gold and other minerals

scholar a person of great learning

volunteers people who offer to do something for someone else

INDEX